#3.4 8791

ISLAM AND THE MUSLIM WORLD

No. 13

General Editor : JOHN RALPH WILLIS
Centre of West African Studies, University of Birmingham

ORIENTAL MYSTICISM

ORIENTAL MYSTICISM

A TREATISE ON

Sufiistic and Unitarian Theosophy
of the Persians

COMPILED FROM NATIVE SOURCES

BY

Edward Henry

E. H. PALMER

FRANK CASS & CO. LTD.

1969

Published by
FRANK CASS AND COMPANY LIMITED
67 Great Russell Street, London WC1

First published   1867
Reprint with a new introduction   1938
Reprint of the First edition   1969

SBN 7146 2264 8

Printed in Great Britain by Clarke, Doble & Brendon Ltd.
Plymouth and London

TO

HIS IMPERIAL MAJESTY,

THE EMPEROR OF THE FRENCH.

الحمد لله

ظلّ سبحاني كيوان همم مريخ حشم خورشيد علم قمر خدم
برجيس شيم عطارد رقم سليمان مكان. NAPOLEON III.
شهنشاه جمجاه فرانسه، عدل افزا ظلم كاه خلّد الله
ملكه و سلطنته

بموقف عرض باريابان.
ازانجا كه همّت والا نهمت آن قدر قدرت براى
ترقّي السنه شرقيه در ممالك محروسه خود به نظر
فوايد و منافع كثير خاص و عام متوجّه است اين
هيچميرز ذرّه بيمقدار را جرات تكريس و تقديس
اين رساله وجيزه بنام نامي ملاذمان عالي آن

شهنشاه اعظم مستجمع الفضایل گردیده که باعث زیاده تر
نیکنامی وشهرت آن اعلی حضرت در هفت کشور
و تالیف قلوب شعرا و فلاسفه و علمای شرق متصور
از یاوری بخت بیدار این خاکسار سیر مدارس عالیه
و کتب خانجات جلیله که برای تحصیل و تکمیل السنهٔ
شرقیه در قلمرو فرانسه اند کرده و معلمان زبدهٔ عصر
و مدرسان علامهٔ دهر که در آن درس میدهند
مشرف به زیارت اوشان شده اسم مبارک آن
تاجدار بحر و بر تا یوم حشر بر زبان فاضلان زمان
بنام نیک مشهور و معروف خواهد بود که آستان
فیض نشان آن نوشیروان دوران داغ نه ناصیهٔ
سر کشان جهان کشای و جهان پرور و جهان
ارای حامی و قدردان اهل فضایل و معاون و
موید تربیت و بهبودی رعایا برایا بوده منجمله
ان السنهٔ شرقیه را از حضیض انقلاب بر آورده
بر اوج ترقی و مباهی در افق یورپ سر بلند
کرده الهی افتاب دولت قوی شوکت و حشمت
ابد مدت و ماهتاب سعادت آن شاهنشاه عادل

علي الدّوام از مطلع جلالت ساطع باد زياده حدّ ادب

:. فقط .:

عرض

فدوي احقر كهتر

E. H. PALMER,
St John's College,
Cambridge.

مورّخهٔ جنوری ســـــنه عيسوي ١٨٩٧

مطابق رمضان ســـــنه هجري ١٣١٥

TRANSLATION.

SIRE,

From a feeling of profound admiration
for the munificent encouragement given to Oriental
studies throughout YOUR MAJESTY's Empire, I have
solicited the honour of dedicating to YOUR MAJESTY
this attempt to contribute towards a better understanding of the Philosopher Poets of the East. The
noble Institutions of France for the promotion of

those studies (some of which it has been my privilege to attend), and the Illustrious Names that adorn them, will make YOUR MAJESTY'S reign long remembered as the brightest Era in European Orientalism.

I have the honour to remain,

SIRE,

YOUR MAJESTY'S

most obedient and humble Servant,

E. H. PALMER.

Dated RAMAZAN, 1283 A.H.
(*January*, 1867, A.D.)

PREFACE.

THE following work is founded upon a Persian MS. treatise by 'Azíz bin Mohammed Nafasí[1], but I have endeavoured to give a clearer and more succinct account of the system than would have been afforded by a mere translation. The term Súfí is derived from the Arabic word *súf* "wool," in allusion to the dress adopted by the Dervishes, who are the master and teachers of the sect; the similarity to the Greek σοφὸς appears to be merely accidental. The system of the Sufis consists in endeavouring

---

[1] The *Maksad i Aksá* or "Remotest Aim." Vide *Hajji Khalfa*, ed. Flügel, Vol. VI. p. 90. This work was originally written in Turkish and translated into Persian by Khwárazím Shah. Some fragments of it were edited in Turkish and Latin by A. Müller, Brandenburg, 1663. The copy I have made use of forms part of a volume containing miscellaneous Persian and Turkish treatises on Philosophical and Religious subjects, presented by Adam Bowen to the Library of Trinity College, Cambridge. It is marked R. 13. 32. in the Catalogue.

to reconcile Philosophy with Revealed Religion, and in assigning a mystical and allegorical interpretation to all religious doctrines and precepts. These tenets are found principally among the Shi'ites, or followers of 'Ali, and appear to have existed in Islamism from its very foundation; indeed the expression of the Corán, "I am the Truth" (Hacc), is the first principle of the system. They may be considered as forming the esoteric doctrine of that creed[1]. Steering a mid course between the pantheism of India on the one hand and the deism of the Corán on the other, the Sufis' cult is the religion of beauty, where heavenly perfection is considered under the imperfect type of earthly loveliness. Their principal writers are the lyric poets, whose aim is to elevate mankind to the contemplation of spiritual things, through the medium of their most impressionable feelings. This habit of contemplation, which is so constantly inculcated by them, requiring as it does retirement and seclusion for its due exercise, inclines the followers of the system somewhat towards asceticism, but in countries where luxury is the idol of the many, we may not unnaturally look

[1] Cf. *La Poesie philosophique et religieuse chez les Persans*, par M. Garcin de Tassy, p. 3.

for a protest against it in the tendencies of the few. My present intention is merely to give an exposition of the system; its origin and history I reserve for a future work, in which I hope to prove that Sufiism is really the development of the Primæval Religion of the Aryan race. The *Ahl i wahdat* form a branch of Sufiism, rather than a separate sect of Theosophists; they insist upon the Universality and Unity of God. I have translated the title "Unitarian," although I am sensible that misapprehension may arise in consequence of its current application to the professors of a particular form of modern belief. I should have preferred the use of some such term as *Monopantachists* had I possessed sufficient courage or position to warrant me in coining so formidable an epithet. The term may be generally understood of those Mussulmans, who, though pursuing philosophical enquiry, refuse to subscribe unreservedly to all the metaphysical doctrines of the Súfís.

The expression *zát i Khudá,* "the Nature of God," by which the Persians designate the very essence and being of the Deity, would, perhaps (according to the general use of the word *zát* in construction with a proper name), be more idiomatically rendered "God Himself;" but as this treatise professes to deal in exactitudes investigated from an Oriental point of view, I have preferred keeping to the original idiom as more definitely expressing the idea.

In conclusion, I have only to acknowledge my obligation to Mr C. A. Hope, of St John's College, for his valuable assistance afforded me in preparing this book for the press.

E. H. PALMER.

St John's College, Cambridge.

CONTENTS.

PART IV.

PART V.

THE STUDY OF MAN.

ORIENTAL MYSTICISM.

Thy prayer-mat stain with wine, if so
The Magian's favour thou canst win,
For travellers in the land should know
The ways and customs of the inn.

HÁFIZ.

THE verse above quoted, like most Oriental poetic writings, is susceptible of a mystical and much higher interpretation than appears from a merely superficial perusal. It is peculiarly illustrative of the allegorical form under which the intellectual life of the Religious Philosopher is treated by the Persians, namely that of a journey, the ultimate object of which is the knowledge of the Infinite Majesty of God; a plan similar to that adopted with reference to the moral life by our own John Bunyan in the Pilgrim's Progress. At the outset of their treatises the term Traveller is applied to the intellectual man only, but the word is afterwards used in a more

general sense, just as in Christian writings man is
not unfrequently called a Wayfarer; it becomes often
identical with Disciple.   M. Garcin de Tassy, in a
work already referred to in the preface, has very
appropriately quoted a verse of St Thomas illustrating this point:

> Ecce panis angelorum
> Factus cibus *viatorum.*

To an elucidation of this system, and the technical
terms employed therein, the following pages are devoted; but to avoid breaking the continuity of the
account, I have endeavoured to present an epitome
of the Oriental Mystic Philosophy from the point of
view taken by the Mohammedan writers, from whom
my information is chiefly derived.   I must therefore
premise that any dogmatical statements that may
occur in the course of the work are not to be considered as enunciations of my own opinion, but as an
exposition of the views of those whose system I am
attempting to expound.

The first part will contain an explanation of, 1,
The terms Traveller, Road, Inns or Stages, and Goal.
2, The words Law, Doctrine, Truth, and the Perfect
Man, according to the Oriental definition of them.
3, What is meant by Fellowship, Renunciation, Attraction and Devotion.

The second, the Sufiistic account of, 1, The Nature; 2, The Attributes; 3, The Works of God; 4, The Four Universal Sources.

The third, a definition of, 1, The Saintly; 2, The Prophetic Office.

The fourth, a dissertation on the Influence of Early Prejudice upon Belief.

The fifth, the Study of Man.

For the benefit of those who study oriental poetry I have added an Appendix, containing a glossary of allegorical and technical terms in use among the Sufiistic writers.

PART I.

CHAPTER I.

OF THE TRAVELLER, THE GOAL, THE STAGES, AND THE ROAD.

The Traveller.

THE Traveller in the path of mystic philosophy is the Perceptive Sense, which as it becomes further developed results in Intelligence, not however the intelligence of life, but such as is described in the words of Mohammed, "Intelligence is light in the heart, distinguishing between truth and vanity, not the intelligence of life." After a time our traveller merges into Divine Light, but of the thousands who start upon the road scarcely one attains thereunto.

The Goal.

The Goal is the Knowledge of God, and the acquisition of this knowledge is the work of Divine Light alone, Perception or worldly intelligence having no lot or portion therein. The latter is represented as the sovereign of this world, and the perceptive faculties are the executive officers of his rule, to whom both the cultivation and devastation of the face of the earth is due. The idea is suggested by the following passage of the Corán: "When God said to the angels, I am about to place a vicegerent in the earth, they said, Wilt thou place therein one who shall commit abomination and shed blood? Nay; we celebrate Thy praise and holiness. God answered them, Verily I know what ye wot not of." (Cor. cap. 2, v. 28.) Which answer implies that God knew that although such might even be the conduct of the bulk of mankind, there would still be some who should receive the Divine Light and attain to a knowledge of Him; so that it is clear that the object of the creation of existent beings was that God should be known. Existence was made for man, and man for the knowledge of God. To the same purport is the answer given to David, "David enquired and said, Oh Lord! why hast thou created mankind? God said, I am a hidden treasure, and I would fain become known[1]." The business of the Traveller then is to exert himself and strive to attain to the Divine light, and so to the knowledge of God; and this is to be achieved by associating with the wise. The received notion of the "stages" in the "road," involves a paradox, the disciple who asks concerning them being told that there is not even a single stage, nay more, not even a road at all. This statement is differently explained by two sects, the Sufis and the *Ahl i Wahdat*, whom I shall call the Unitarians. The Sufis say that there is no road from man to God, because the nature of God is illimitable and infinite, without beginning or end or even direction. There is not a single atom of existent things with which

Object of Philosophical Inquiry.

The stages and the road.

---

[1] Cf. Sale's Coran, Preliminary Discourse, p. 97.

God is not and which God does not comprise: "Are
they not in doubt concerning the union with their
Lord? doth he not comprise everything?" (Cor. cap.
42, v. 54.) Nor is there aught that he does not comprehend with his knowledge: "Verily God compre-
hendeth all things with his knowledge." (Cor. cap.
42, v. 54.) The Traveller who has not attained to
this Divine Light can have no lot or portion with
God, but those who have reached it gaze always
upon His face; they go not forth by day and retire
not to rest at night without an abashed consciousness
that God is present every where; for with Him they
live, and in Him they act.

The whole universe compared with the majesty
of God is as a drop in the ocean, nay infinitely less
than this. But Perception or Intelligence can never
lead to this conviction, or reveal this glorious mystery; that is the province of the Divine Light alone.
Such is the Sufiistic explanation of the proposition,
"There is no road from man to God."

Unitarian
Interpreta-
tion of the
preceding.
The Unitarians interpret it as follows. They
hold that existence is not independent, but is of God;
that besides the existence of God there is no real
existence, nor can there possibly be: for that which
exists not, cannot exist of itself, but that which does
exist, exists of itself, and that which is self-existent is
God.

When man imagines that he has an existence
other than the existence of God he falls into a griev-
ous error and sin; yet this error and sin is the only
road from man to God; for until the Traveller has

passed over this he cannot reach God. A certain
Sufi poet has said,

> Plant one foot on the neck of self,
> The other in thy Friend's domain;
> In everything His presence see,
> For other vision is in vain.

That is, whilst you are looking up to self you cannot
see God, but when you are not looking up to self all
that you see is God. Such is the Unitarian solution
of the proposition that "there is no road from man
to God," namely that the error of imagining an existence separate from God is the only road to Him;
the stages on this road are innumerable, and some
philosophers even assert that it has no end.

CHAPTER II.

OF LAW, DOCTRINE AND TRUTH.

THE Law is the word of the Prophet, the Doctrine
is the example of the Prophet, and the Truth is the
vision of the Prophet. This follows from the Hadís[1],
"My words are Law, my example is Doctrine, my
state is Truth." The Traveller must first learn the
theory of the Law, and act up to the practice of the
Doctrine, by which means the Truth will become
manifest in him. Those who possess all these three
things are the Perfect, and these are the leaders
of the people; but those who are deficient in all
are lower than the brutes; these are the wretches

Definition of Law, Doctrine and Truth.

---

[1] The sayings of Mohammed are so called.

referred to in the Coran: "Verily we have created
for Hell many of mankind and of the genii; hearts
have they and understand not, eyes have they and
see not, ears have they and hear not; they are like
unto the beasts of the field, nay more perverse, for
they are the negligent." (Cor. cap. 7, v. 178.) From
this we learn that each is bound to fulfil his duty
in his allotted sphere.

Of the superficial and the real.

The superficial has no credit without the real.
Mankind in reality is man; the animal kingdom in
reality is animal. By reality is meant the possession
and employment of the qualities naturally appertain-
ing to the order to which the individual belongs.
Thus the wise man knows all, sees all, and works
with all; for otherwise the business of the world
would not go on. Teachers also work in their way
for the same reason. But Rulers work not, or otherwise the harmony of the world would be disturbed.

The object of Law, Doctrine and Truth.

The final object of Law, Doctrine and Truth
is that mankind should speak aright, act aright, and
think aright, or, in other words, become wise and
good. The object is threefold: first, that man may
not become like the brute he should receive the
command and prohibition of Scripture, and obey the
same. This he must confirm in his heart and confess
with his tongue. Secondly, that he may be adorned
with grace and piety he should associate with the
wise, and strive earnestly to know and understand
the unity of God. Thirdly, that he may become
accomplished he should, after the knowledge of God,
learn the nature and properties of material objects.

When thus accomplished the Traveller may be considered as adorned with Law, Doctrine and Truth.

But all the foregoing theory is useless without practice; the Traveller cannot arrive at the goal unless he combines theory with practice, superficiality with reality; for the Coran says, " and righteous actions shall raise him." (Cor. cap. 35, v. 11.) Now the actions constituting this practice are ten in number. 1. Search after God, which is the object of all striving and conflict. 2. Search after Wisdom, the guide without whom it is impossible to find the road. 3. Inclination towards the wise ; that is, the Traveller should frequent the society of the wise and sit as a disciple at their feet. This inclination is the strong steed that bears him on his way. 4. Obedience. The Traveller should in everything be obedient and submissive to the wise, both in reference to the affairs of this world and the next. 5. Renunciation. He must renounce trifling, and at the bidding of the elder even give up all that he has to his care, forsaking his most favourite pursuits, unless they meet with the approbation of his superior. 6. Piety. He must be pious and continent, in word and deed and mode of life, complying with the dictates of the Law and the Scriptures. 7. Submission. The serenity of the Traveller's path is the result of submission to the Law. 8. Reticence. To speak little. 9. Vigilance. To sleep little. 10. Temperance. To eat little. These are the marks which determine the practice of the followers of the Doctrine, ten fierce dragons in the Traveller's path to keep him from

swerving in the direction of sin. If he assiduously
follow them under the direction of the wise he ultimately reaches his Goal, and the Truth is made manifest in him; but if he be deficient in one only
he can never arrive at his destination.

Marks and Practice of the followers of Truth.

There are also ten marks which determine the
practice of the followers of Truth. 1. That the
Traveller should know God first, and subsequently the
nature and properties of material objects. 2. That
he should be at peace with all the world, and refrain
from all contradiction and opposition. According to
the mother from whom he is born into the community
each receives a different patronymic; thus one is
called a Hanefite, one a Shaffiite[1], one a Pagan, one a
Jew, and another a Mussulmán; but the true philosopher recognises in each a weak and helpless being
like himself, he sees in each a fellow-searcher after
God. 3. Charity towards all. Charity is that course
of action and teaching which benefits our fellows both
temporally and spiritually. Now real charity consists in the employment of counsel and discipline.
Teachers should employ counsel that men may be
improved; rulers should employ discipline for the

[1] The Hanefites are the followers of Abú Hanífa, one of the
principal authorities for the traditional law. His doctrines are
esteemed chiefly among the Turks.

The Shaffiites are those who follow the tenets taught by Abú
Abdallah Mohammed ben Idrís, al Sháfi'í, who was descended from
the family of Mohammed. Salah-uddin (Saladin) founded a college
for the exclusive propagation of his doctrines at Cairo. A beautiful
mosque to his memory also exists at Herát, in Khorassan. Both
sects are considered perfectly orthodox by the Mussulmáns.

regulation and well-being of society. 4. Humility; this consists in paying due respect to others. 5. Submission and resignation. 6. Trust in God, patience, endurance and perseverance. 7. Freedom from avarice; for avarice is the mother of vice. 8. Contentment. 9. Inoffensiveness. 10. Conviction; for the Truth brings conviction with it.

Such are the marks, and such is the practice of the followers of Truth; and until the Traveller shall have thoroughly penetrated the inmost depths of wisdom, and shall have completed the journey to and in God, these marks and qualities will not be made manifest in him.

CHAPTER III.

CONCERNING THE PERFECT MAN, AND THE PERFECTLY FREE MAN.

THE Perfect Man is he who has fully comprehended the Law, the Doctrine and the Truth; or, in other words, he who is endued with four things in perfection; viz. 1. Good words; 2. Good deeds; 3. Good principles; 4. The sciences. It is the business of the Traveller to provide himself with these things in perfection, and by so doing he will provide himself with perfection. *The Perfect Man.*

The Perfect Man has had various other names assigned to him, all equally applicable, viz. Elder, Leader, Guide, Inspired Teacher, Wise, Virtuous, Perfect, Perfecter, [1]Beacon and Mirror of the world, *Other titles applied to him.*

---

[1] In Persian *Jám i Jehán numá*, the fabled cup of Jemshíd, in

Powerful Antidote, Mighty Elixir, 'Isà the Raiser of the Dead, Khizar the Discoverer of the Water of Life, and Solomon who knew the language of Birds.

The Universe has been likened to a single person, of whom the Perfect Man is the Soul; and again, to a tree, of which mankind is the fruit, and the Perfect Man the pith and essence. Nothing is hidden from the Perfect Man; for after arriving at the knowledge of God, he has attained to that of the nature and properties of material objects, and can henceforth find no better employment than acting mercifully towards mankind. Now there is no mercy better than to devote oneself to the perfection and improvement of others, both by precept and example. Thus the Prophet is called in the Coran "a mercy to the Universe." (Cor. cap. 21, v. 107.) But with all his perfection the Perfect Man cannot compass his desires, but passes his life in consistent and unavoidable self-denial: he is perfect in knowledge and principle, but imperfect in faculty and power.

His business.

There have indeed been Perfect Men possessed of power; such power as that which resides in kings and rulers; yet a careful consideration of the poor extent of man's capacities will shew that his weakness is preferable to his power, his want of faculty preferable to his possession of it. Prophets and saints, kings and sultans, have desired many things, and failed to obtain them; they have wished to avoid

Perfection not incompatible with Power.

which were reflected all passing events; and *'Aina e Jehán-numá*, the mirror of Alexander the Great, said to have possessed the same singular properties.

many things, and have had them forced upon them. Mankind is made up of the Perfect and the Imperfect, of the Wise and the Foolish, of Kings and Subjects, but all are alike weak and helpless, all pass their lives in a manner contrary to their desires; this the Perfect Man recognises and acts upon, and, knowing that nothing is better for man than renunciation, forsakes all and becomes free and at leisure. As before he renounced wealth and dignity, so now he foregoes eldership and teachership, esteeming freedom and rest above everything: the fact is, that though the motive alleged for education and care of others is a feeling of compassion and a regard for discipline, yet the real instigation is the love of dignity: as the Prophet says, "The last thing that is removed from the chiefs of the righteous is love of dignity." I have said that the Perfect Man should *The Perfectly Free Man.* be endued with four things in perfection: now the Perfectly Free Man should have four additional characteristics, viz. renunciation, retirement, contentment, and leisure. He who has the first four is virtuous, but not free: he who has the whole eight is perfect, liberal, virtuous, and free. Furthermore, there are two grades of the Perfectly Free—those *The two grades of the Perfectly Free.* who have renounced wealth and dignity only, and those who have further renounced eldership and teachership, thus becoming free and at leisure. These again are subdivided into two classes; those who, after renunciation, retirement and contentment, make choice of obscurity, and those who, after renunciation, make choice of submission, contemplation and resig-

nation; but the object of both is the same. Some
writers assert that freedom and leisure consists in
the former course, while others maintain that it is
only to be found in the latter.

Those who make choice of obscurity are actuated
by the knowledge that annoyance and distraction of
thought are the invariable concomitants of society;
they therefore avoid receiving visits and presents,
and fear them as they would venomous beasts. The
other class, who adopt submission, resignation and
contemplation, do so because they perceive that
mankind for the most part are ignorant of what is
good for them, being dissatisfied with what is bene-
ficial, and delighted with circumstances that are
harmful to them; as the Coran says, "Perchance ye
may dislike what is good for you, and like what is
hurtful to you." (Cor. cap. 2, v. 213.) For this reason they retire from society equally with the other
class, caring little what the world may think of them.
The eminent Sufis are divided in opinion as to which
of these two courses is to be preferred.

CHAPTER IV.

CONCERNING FELLOWSHIP AND RENUNCIATION.

Fellow-
ship.

FELLOWSHIP has many qualities and effects both of
good and evil. The fellowship of the wise is the
only thing that can conduct the Traveller safely to
the Goal; therefore all the submission, earnestness
and discipline that have been hitherto inculcated
are merely in order to render him worthy of such

fellowship. Provided he have the capacity, a single day, nay, a single hour, in the society of the wise, tends more to his improvement than years of self-discipline without it. "Verily one day with thy Lord is better than a thousand years." (Cor. cap. 22, v. 46.)

It is however possible to frequent the society of the wise without receiving any benefit therefrom, but this must proceed either from want of capacity or want of will. In order then to avoid such a result, the Sufis have laid down the following rules for the conduct of the disciple when in the presence of his teachers.

Hear, attend, but speak little.

Never answer a question not addressed to you; but if asked, answer promptly and concisely, never feeling ashamed to say, "I know not."

Do not dispute for disputation's sake.

Never boast before your elders.

Never seek the highest place, nor even accept it if it be offered to you.

Do not be over-ceremonious, for this will compel your elders to act in the same manner towards you, and give them needless annoyance.

Observe in all cases the etiquette appropriate to the time, place and persons present.

In indifferent matters, that is, matters involving no breach of duty by their omission or commission, conform to the practice and wishes of those with whom you are associating.

Rules to be observed in intercourse with Elders.

Do not make a practice of anything which is not
either a duty or calculated to increase the com-
fort of your associates; otherwise it will become
an idol to you; and it is incumbent on every one
to break his idols and renounce his habits.

Renuncia-
tion.

This leads us to the subject of Renunciation,
which is of two kinds, external and internal. The
former is the renunciation of worldly wealth; the
latter, the renunciation of worldly desires. Everything that hinders or veils the Traveller's path must
be renounced, whether it relate to this world or the
next. Wealth and dignity are great hindrances;
but too much praying and fasting are often hindrances too. The one is a shroud of darkness, the
other a veil of light. The Traveller must renounce
idolatry, if he desire to reach the Goal, and everything that bars his progress is an idol. All men
have some idol, which they worship; with one it is
wealth and dignity, with another overmuch prayer
and fasting. If a man sit always upon his prayer-
carpet his prayer-carpet becomes his idol. And so
on with a great number of instances.

What
ought and
what
ought not
to be re-
nounced.

Renunciation must not be performed without the
advice and permission of an elder. It should be the
renunciation of trifles, not of necessaries, such as
food, clothing and dwelling-place, which are indispensable to man; for without them he would be
obliged to rely on the aid of others, and this would
beget avarice, which is "the mother of vice." The
renunciation of necessaries produces as corrupting

an influence upon the mind as the possession of too much wealth. The greatest of blessings is to have a sufficiency, but to over-step this limit is to gain nought but additional trouble.

Renunciation is the practice of those who know God, and the characteristic mark of the wise. Every individual fancies that he alone possesses this knowledge, but knowledge is an attribute of the mind, and there is no approach from unaided sense to the attributes of the mind, by which we can discover who is, or who is not, possessed of this knowledge. Qualities however are the sources of action; therefore a man's practice is an infallible indication of the qualities he possesses; if, for instance, a man asserts that he is a baker, a carpenter, or a blacksmith, we can judge at once if he possesses skill in these crafts by the perfection of his handiwork. In a word, theory is internal, and practice external, the presence of the practice, therefore, is a proof that the theory too is there.

Renunciation how recognized.

Renunciation is necessary to the real confession of faith ; for the formula "There is no God but God," involves two things, negation and proof. Negation is the renunciation of other Gods, and proof is the knowledge of God. Wealth and dignity have led many from the right path, they are the gods the people worship ; if then you see that one has renounced these, you may be sure that he has expelled the love of this world from his heart, and completed the negation ; and whosoever has attained to the knowledge of God has completed the proofs.

Application of this test.

This is really confessing that "there is no God but God;" and he who has not attained to the knowledge of God, has never really repeated the confession of faith. Early prejudices are a great stumblingblock to many people; for the first principles of Mono-theism are contained in the words of the Hadís: "Every one is born with a disposition [for the true faith], but his parents make him a Jew, a Christian, or a Magian." The Unitarians also say, that the real confession of faith consists in negation and proof; but they explain negation by renunciation of self, and proof by acknowledgement of God.

Conclu-
sion.   Thus, according to the Sufis, confession of faith, prayer and fasting contain two distinct features, namely, form and truth; the former being entirely inefficacious without the latter. Renunciation and the knowledge of God are like a tree; the know-ledge of God is the root, renunciation the branches, and all good principles and qualities are the fruit. To sum up, the lesson to be learnt is that in repeat-ing the formula the Traveller must acknowledge in his heart that God only always was, God only al-ways will be. This world and the next, nay, the very existence of the Traveller, may vanish, but God alone remains. This is the true confession of faith ; and although the Traveller before was blind, the moment he is assured of this his eyes are opened, and he seeth.

CHAPTER V.

CONCERNING ATTRACTION AND DEVOTION.

The Sufis hold that there are three aids necessary to conduct the Traveller on his path.

1. Attraction ; 2. Devotion ; 3. Elevation.

Attraction is the act of God, who draws man towards Himself. Man sets his face towards this world, and is entangled in the love of wealth and dignity, until the grace of God steps in and turns his heart towards God. The tendency proceeding from God is called Attraction; that which proceeds from man is called Inclination, Desire and Love. As the inclination increases, its name changes, and it causes the Traveller to renounce everything else becoming a Kiblah, to set his face towards God ; when it has become his Kiblah, and made him forget everything but God, it is developed into Love. *Attraction.*

Inclination defined.

Most men when they have attained this stage are content to pass their lives therein, and leave the world without making further progress. Such a person the Sufis call Attracted (مجذوب).

Others, however, proceed from this to self-examination, and pass the rest of their lives in devotion. They are then called Devoutly Attracted (مجذوبِسالك). If devotion be first practised, and the attraction of God then step in, such a person is called an Attracted Devotee (سالكمجذوب). If **he practise and complete devotion, but is not**

influenced by the attraction of God, he is called a
Devotee (سالك).

Sheikh Sheháb-uddín[1], in his work entitled *'Awá
rif al Ma'árif,* says that an elder or teacher should
be selected from the second class alone; for although
many may be estimable and righteous, it is but few
who are fit for such offices, or for the education of
disciples[2].

Devotion.   Devotion is the prosecution of the journey, and
that in two ways, to God and in God. The first,
the Sufis say, has a limit; the second is boundless;
the journey to God is completed when the Traveller
has attained to the knowledge of God; and then
commences the journey in God, which has for its
object the knowledge of the Nature and Attributes
of God; a task which they confess is not to be accomplished in so short a space as the lifetime of man.

> The knowledge wisest men have shared
>   Of Thy great power and Thee
> Is less, when with Thyself compared,
>   Than one drop in a sea.

The Unitarians maintain that the journey to God
is completed when the Traveller has acknowledged
that there is no existence save that of God; the
journey in God they explain to be a subsequent
inquiry into the mysteries of nature.

[1] Shiháb-ud-dín Abu Hafs Omar bin Mohammed bin Abdallah,
Soharawerdí, died A.D. 1106. See *Hajji Khalfa,* Vol. IV. p. 275.

[2] مريد *muríd* is properly one who possesses the Inclination
ارادة before mentioned.

The term Elevation or ascent (عروج) is almost synonymous with Progress, and will be explained in that part of the work which treats of the study of Man.

Elevation or Ascent.

CHAPTER VI.

CONCERNING COUNSEL.

ALL counsel may be summed up in the simple words, My friend, rely not on life, health, or riches. Nothing over which the firmament of heaven revolves maintains an unchanged existence, but every hour assumes some new form. Every moment a fresh picture is presented to the view; and one appearance is scarce complete ere another supervenes, obliterating all traces of the first, as wave follows wave upon the shore. No wise man would seek to build his house upon the waves, or hope to find a foundation for it there. To quote the words of Hafiz:

Counsel.

> In hope's unstable palace no foundations shalt thou find,
> Then seize the passing hour, for life but rests upon the wind.

The wisest of mankind are those who have renounced all worldly desires, and chosen the calm and peaceful lot of a recluse's life. Behind every pleasure lurk twenty pains; far better is it then to forego one fleeting joy and spare oneself a lifetime of regret. Life, health, riches, and happiness, may be our portion to-day; but God alone knows what the morrow may bring forth.

PART II.

CHAPTER I.

CONCERNING THE NATURE OF GOD.

The neces-sity for a Creator recognized. THE Sufis consider it an axiom that the world must have had a Creator. They affirm that He is One, Ancient, First and Last, the End and Limit of all things, Incomparable, Unchangeable, Indivisible, and Immaterial, not subject to the laws of time, place or direction; possessing the attributes of holiness, and exempt from all opposite qualities. In this

Sufiistic account of His Na-ture. their account agrees with the opinion of the Oriental thinking world in general; but they further assert that He is Infinite and Illimitable, by which they mean not only without beginning or end, but also without determinate position of time, place, or di-rection. The Nature of God, according to them, is an infinite and illimitable light, a boundless and fathomless Ocean, compared with which the entire universe is more insignificant than a drop of water

His Omni-presence. in the sea. There is no single atom of existent beings which God does not pervade, comprise and comprehend. God is always near to man, but man is always far from God, because he is not aware of His proximity. The proximity of God to all created His prox- beings is the same, for the highest and lowest are imity alike in His sight. The light of God is the only thing that can reveal this proximity to the Traveller.

There are three grades of proximity to God which are out of the reach of human Intelligence: the proximity of Time, Place and Attributes. We can say, for instance, that Mohammed was nearer our own time than Christ; that the moon is nearer to the earth than the planet Jupiter; that Báyazíd Bístámí[1] more closely resembled Mohammed in qualities than did any even of the Prophet's contemporaries ; but we cannot predicate this proximity of God. The verse of the Coran, "He is with you wherever you are" (Cor. cap. 57, v. 4), alludes to this mysterious proximity. Intelligence has no road to the dis- discover- covery of it, but when its majesty has overshadowed able only the Illuminati, they perceive that in the sight of God by the In- itiated. Saints and Prophets, unbelievers and heretics, the loftiest of mankind and the meanest of brutes, are alike compared with Him. This is their explanation of the passage "Thou wilt see no distinction in the Creation of the Merciful One" (Cor. cap. 67, v. 3), and "God's is the East and the West, and wherever you turn your faces God is there." (Cor. cap. 2, v. 109.)

The Traveller who has discovered this proximity possesses the one thing needful, and has completed the journey to God, but until he shall have over-

---

[1] An eminent Sufí philosopher and poet. See Sprenger, *Journal As. S. of Bengal*, 1856, p. 134.

come the restraints of time and place his steps can
never border on the threshold of Eternity. Eter-
Eternity. nity, in the Sufiistic sense, is the primal element of
Cosmos, and takes in at one glance both past and
future time. This idea is contained in the words of
the Hadís: "There is no morning or evening with
thy Lord." The passage in the Coran "Oh assembly
of genii and men! if ye are able to pass out of the
confines of Heaven, then pass out of them; but ye
will do so only by the authority which God giveth
you," (Cor. cap. 55, v. 33), points to the Majesty of
Him of whose proximity we are speaking.

Solution of   This Sufiistic account of the nature and prox-
Questions
arising out imity of God gives rise to many questions amongst
of the Sufi- their disciples. For instance, "In what way is the
istic ac-
count. nature of God infinite and illimitable, in reference
to the sensible and invisible world separately considered?" The answer, however, follows plainly from
the previous statements. For since the nature of
God is infinite and illimitable, and no notion of time,
place, or direction attaches to it, it is equally above
the highest conception of the invisible world, and
below the lowest material object of the sensible
world. Again, their statement concerning the proximity of God to all things alike, and His comprising
and comprehending all things, seems irreconcileable
with any conception that human intelligence can
form of His Nature. This objection they meet by
the following physical illustration.

Physical   Earth is dense, water compared with earth is
illustration subtle, air is more subtle than water, fire is more

subtle than air; and the subtle occupies a higher of the fore-
position in the scale of creation than the dense. going position.
Now although each of these four elements occupies a
distinct position in nature they are susceptible of
commixture, and are determined the one by the other.
If, for instance, a vessel be completely filled with
earth there will still be space for water, and when it
will contain no more water it will still admit of the
introduction of air, and when it will contain no more
air it will still admit of the introduction of fire ; the
comprehensive and penetrating capacities of each being in proportion to their relative densities.   It will
now be observed that there is no particle of the earth
in the vessel but is commingled with the water, and
so on of the other three elements, each occupying its
distinct and proper position according to its density.
It is from the proper gradation and arrangement of
these four elements in the world that the phenomena
of nature arise ; but they are nevertheless susceptible of commixture and conjunction.   This again may
be proved by experiment.   If one thrust his hand
into water it is moistened and not burnt, if into fire
it is burnt and not moistened, but if he thrust it into
boiling water it is both moistened and burnt, thereby
proving that these two elements are susceptible of
commixture and conjunction.   That the four elements do occupy their distinct and proper positions
in nature, is evident from the premises concerning
their relative densities, for the denser cannot disturb
or confine the more subtle.   If all this be possible
then in the case of material elements, how much

more possible is it in the case of the nature of God, which is immaterial and indivisible!

Further illustration of the same from psychology.

Another and closer illustration is that taken from the connection of the human soul with the body. The soul is conjoined with the body, and does not merely reside in it; so that there is no atom of the corporeal frame distinct from or not pervaded, comprised and comprehended by it. The limbs may be separated one by one, and the body itself even cut into pieces without any wound or hurt accruing to the soul; for the body, which is the denser of the two, cannot disturb or confine the soul, which is the more subtle. In like manner the Nature of God pervades, comprises and comprehends everything, and is incapable of being disturbed or confined by anything.

The Subtle Nature of God.

Again, since the Nature of God is infinitely subtle, nothing can ever veil or conceal it; for the more subtle a thing is the greater is its capacity for penetration. Thus the Sufis explain the expression of the Coran, "He is the Subtle the Wise[1]," with reference to the Nature of God, as the only truly subtle nature. They say that this sentence would convince every one of the truth of the Mohammedan creed if they could but understand that this is the right interpretation of it. This proximity of God is implied in the

---

[1] وهو اللّطيف الخبير. (Cor. cap. 6, v. 103). In Sale's version the word *latíf* is rendered *gracious*. I have, however, translated it *subtle*, which is its primary meaning, and accords with the Sufiistic interpretation.

verses, "He is with you wherever you are; God
seeth all that ye do" (Cor. cap. 57, v. 4). "I am
nearer to him than his jugular vein" (Cor. cap. 50,
v. 15). And many similar passages both of the Corán
and the Hadís.

The foregoing arguments are intended specially Object of
to confute the opinion that God is nearer to some these Arguments.
men than others, namely, that the Wise approach
nearer to Him than the Ignorant. Their great
object, however, is the inculcation of the beautiful
truth, that He is ever near to those who seek Him,
whilst those only are far from Him who by their
actions fail to acknowledge that He is Omnipresent
and Omniscient, knowing and seeing all they do.

CHAPTER II.

CONCERNING THE ATTRIBUTES OF GOD.

SHEIKH Sadr-ud-dín Rúmí[1] affirms that the Attri- The Distinction
butes and Names of God are convertible terms; but between
Sheikh Sa'ad-ud-dín Hamawí[2] maintains that the Names and
Coran and Hadís contain no synonymous words what- Attributes investigat-
ever, and that it is incompatible with the character of ed.
a Sage to make use of two or more expressions to con-
vey a single meaning. According to him Attributes
are intrinsic and Names descriptive; the former
relating to the Nature, the latter to the Aspect of

[1] Also called El Kúnawí. Vide *Hajji Khalfa,* ed. Flügel, Vol. I.
p. 350, &c.
[2] Vide *Hajji Khalfa,* Vol. III. pp. 78, 582.

the being described. Works again relate to the In-
dividuality. This is the opinion generally received
among the Súfís. Sheikh Sadr-ud-dín, on the other
hand, maintains that the Attributes of God are from
one point themselves the Nature of God, and are
contrary to it from another. They are themselves
the Nature of God in this way, that where there is
no existence save His Nature, His Attributes must
of necessity be His Nature also. They are contrary
to it in this way, that as things understood are necessarily various, the names used to express them must
be various too, and must imply distinctions of meaning and idea. But all distinction and divisibility is
contrary to the Nature of God.

Classifica-
tion of the
Attri-
butes.

The names applied to God, of Living, Eternal,
Author or Disposer, and Omnipotent, imply His
Eternal and Abiding Nature; actual names according to the Mohammedan theory having existed prior
to their meanings[1]. Such expressions therefore are
the names of the actual names, and are called Posi-
tive Attributes. These names are called the four
pillars of Divinity. Such names however as The
Exalter and Debaser, The Giver of Life and Death,
refer to attendant powers, and are called Relative
Attributes. Lastly, such names as The Blameless,
The Holy One, The Independent One, relate to the
absence of imperfection, and are hence called Nega-

---

[1] It must be borne in mind that one of the principal dogmas of
Islám is that the Corán was preexistent to all created things, and
by implication also the Arabic language in which it is written, and
to which the names above mentioned belong.

tive Attributes. All the other names of God may be referred to one or other of these three classes, except the name *Allah* itself[1], which comprises all the attributes of His Eternal and Abiding Nature, for all the other names can be used to qualify it. The name Merciful, occurring in the initiatory formula, " In the name of God the Merciful, the Compassionate," is held in the next greatest reverence, although referring to the outward attributes of God only. The Coran says, "Say, Pray unto God (*Allah*), or pray unto the Merciful One (*Ar Rahmán*). By whichsoever of the two names ye invoke Him it is equal, for to Him belong the best of names." (Cor. cap. 17, v. 110.) All these names collectively or individually indicate One and the same God.

The name Allah.

CHAPTER III.

CONCERNING THE WORKS OF GOD, PHYSICALLY CONSIDERED.

THE Works of God are of two kinds, visible and invisible. The first is the Perceived, the second the Conceived World. The Perceived World is also called The Material, Visible, Created, and Lower World. The Conceived World is spoken of as the Invisible, Spiritual, or Future World, and the World of Command[2]: this division is based on the words,

The Worlds perceived and conceived.

---

[1] The name *Allah* is abbreviated from *Al-Iláh*, "the God" *par excellence.*

[2] الامر. The command of God كن فكان (*kun fa kán*), "be and it was," is here alluded to. The Sufis in their poetry frequently

"Are not creation and command of Him?" (Cor. cap. 7, v. 52.) The material world may be described in detail, but of the spiritual world we must be content with a mere outline, for none but those who have gone hence, and entered into the spiritual life, can know the condition thereof: as Jesus Christ has said, "Except a man be born again he cannot enter into the kingdom of heaven[1]."

Inhabitants of the Invisible World. There are two classes of beings in the Invisible World, those whose existence is revealed in inspiration (كُنْ), and those who make their existence felt

speak of God as the *Lord of káf and nún,* i.e. of the two letters composing the word of command *kun* "be."

[1] ‏لأيلج ملكوت السموات و الارض من لم يولد مرتين‎.

The Mohammedans although denying the Divinity of Our Lord recognize the inspiration of both the Old and New Testaments, which as well as the Apocryphal Gospels they frequently quote as authorities. They even assert that the promise of the Comforter referred to their own prophet, and support their arguments by an ingenious perversion of the text, reading περικλυτὸς for παράκλητος, the former being almost identical in signification with the name of Mohammed (*Multum laudatus*). The charge of inconsistency in not believing in our scriptures they meet by accusing the Christians of having themselves altered many similar portions of the original, and by maintaining that the mission of Mohammed, the Seal of the Prophets as he is called, abrogated all other religions. Thus Sa'adi says in his Bústán:

‏يتيمي كه‌ناكرده قران درست‎
‏كتب‌خانه چند ملت بشست‎

That Perfect one who, ere the whole of Gabriel's book he reads,
Has blotted out the library of all the People's creeds."

(بيان). The first are subdivided into two classes,
namely, Emanations and Agencies. Emanations ^Emana-
are what are addressed in the words of Mohammed, ^tions.
" *Salve !* in the majesty of God, in His Glory which
was before the world began." They are called by
the Mohammedans *Maláïk Muhaymeh,* i.e. Angels
designated by the word *hámú,* " *salve.*" Mohammed
gives the following account of them: " Verily with
the Most High God there is a luminous land, the
sun journeyeth there in 30 days, in an orbit of 30
days, like the days of the world : its creation knows
the Most High God, but there are others in the earth
who know not God, the sons of Adam, and Iblís."

Agencies are, as it were, the door-keepers of ^Agencies.
Divinity, and the means by which God's bounty is
vouchsafed to man. The head and chief of them,
according to the Muslims, is Mohammed, than whom
there is no more exalted spirit. " I have created
nothing more honoured in my sight than thee."

The Holy Spirit, or Gabriel, is, according to them,
the last of this class of agencies, being the actual
and intermediate agent of intercourse between God
and man. " There is not one of us who hath not
his assigned position."

The other beings whose existence is felt are also ^Agents.
subdivided into two classes, namely, Agents and
Powers. The former are the presiding genii, or per-
sonified laws of animal, vegetable and mineral pro-
duction, whence the common saying, " Everything
has its angel." Mohammed himself says, " An angel
descends in every drop of rain or dew," and the mys-

tics assert that God does not create a single leaf upon a tree without the intervention of seven angels. The human soul, though compounded both of the material and the immaterial, is reckoned amongst this class. It is the masterpiece of creation, and the whole material world is placed under its control[1].

Powers.   The Powers who form the second class are the Genii and Devils. They are created of fire, and constitute the lower order of beings in the invisible world. Some of them have a certain power over the race of man granted to them, but are rebellious against the Most High; of these Iblís is the Head and Chief. Others, again, although capable of harm, are subservient to the will of God.

[1] The accompanying table of the Mohammedan Cosmogony may assist the reader in understanding this and the following chapters.

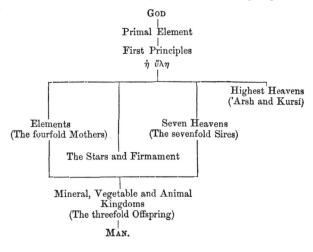

GOD
|
Primal Element
|
First Principles
ἡ ὕλη
|

Elements
(The fourfold Mothers)

Seven Heavens
(The sevenfold Sires)

Highest Heavens
('Arsh and Kursí)

The Stars and Firmament

Mineral, Vegetable and Animal
Kingdoms
(The threefold Offspring)
|
MAN.

The material world is also of two kinds, heavenly and earthly. The heavenly are the Throne and the Seat of God (or the Highest Heavens), the Seven Inferior Heavens, the Firmament and the Stars. The Earthly are the Face of the Earth, the Elements, Signs from on high (as thunder, lightning and rain), Compound Bodies (as minerals, vegetables and animals), the Sea, and other Works of God without end. Such is the Sufiistic account of the works of God, physically considered.

Of the Heavenly and the Earthly.

CHAPTER IV.

CONCERNING THE WORKS OF GOD, METAPHYSICALLY CONSIDERED.

THE first thing that God created was the Primal Element (جوهر اول), that is to say, the primal element of the entire Universe. This according to the Coran He created of Himself without any medium whatever, and in infinitely less space of time than the twinkling of an eye. " And it was not the business of an hour, but even as the twinkling of an eye, or quicker still." (Cor. cap. 16, v. 79.)[1] This Primal Element is designated by various other names, such as the Primal Intelligence, the Constructive Spirit, the Pen, the Mightiest Spirit, the Spirit of Mohammed (or the Laudable Spirit), and the like. It is so excel-

The Primal Element.

---

[1] This passage is differently interpreted by the Arab commentators, and is made to refer to " the business of the last hour;" see Sale's translation.

lent and subtle, that God alone knows its worth. It is the perfection of wisdom and propinquity to God, is ever yearning after Him, and ever present with Him; nor is there anything save this Primal Element that can directly approach Him, or become the direct recipient of His bounty.

The Primal Element is God's world, and the Universe is the world of the Primal Element. By this alone the Voice of God is heard, but its voice is heard throughout the whole Universe, conveying the behests of the Most High[1].

"The Pen." It is the Pen of God which at His command wrote down the Simple Natures, and in the twinkling of an eye they started into being, the Intelligences, Souls, Elements and Natures, the Heavens and the Stars[2]. These then took up the task, and obeyed the second mandate by writing down the compound bodies, and straightway the Mineral, Vegetable and Animal Kingdoms sprung into existence.

This is the explanation of the words which begin the 68th Chapter of the Corán: "N, by the Pen, and what they write." The mystic letter represents the World of Power, the Inkstand[3] of God; the Pen is the Primal Element, and "what they write" refers to the Simple Natures. These are the scribes of God, and the words they write are the compound

---

[1] Cf. Psalm xix. vv. 1—3.

[2] The first two and the Heavens are denominated the Comptrollers: "and the Comptrollers for command." (Cor. cap. 79, v. 5.)

[3] The letter N stands for the word *nún*, which is not only the Arabic name of the letter, but also signifies an inkhorn. Cf. AL BEIDHAWI's commentary.

bódies of nature. They are writing even now, and will write on for ever; for "were the sea ink it would not suffice for the words of my Lord[1]." (Cor. cap. 18, v. 109.)

There are nine heavenly spheres, each higher than the preceding; the highest of all is called the Heaven of Heavens, or the Throne of God (عرش). Each of these spheres possesses a Soul and an Intelligence, higher and more subtle in proportion to their order. The Intelligence of the Heaven of Heavens is called the Primal Intelligence, the Souls and Intelligences which occupy the other eight are identical with the Cherubim and Spirits of the religious account. *The Spheres.*

In point of time they precede the simple Natures above referred to, being eternal, while the latter are casual; in point of mental excellence, however, they rank after them. Their precedence over the Simple Natures is as the precedence of the Sun's Orb over its rays. The next in order of creation are the Threefold Offspring, *i. e.* the Mineral, Vegetable, and Animal Kingdoms. Both the metaphysical and the physical account agree concerning these last, that they are casual; but their account of what are called the Parents[2] differs. *Order of Creation*

---

[1] This idea of the Primal Element appears to have originated partly from a refinement on the ordinary interpretation of the text; "When He willeth aught He but sayeth to it, 'Be, and it is so'," where an undue significance is given to the pronoun *it*.

[2] By these are meant the "seven climes," or "zones," (into which, according to the Mohammedan cosmography, the earth is divided),

Intelligence the beginning and the end.

Because man was the final object of creation, and because when he has attained Intelligence he is complete, and because there is nothing beyond Intelligence, and Primal Intelligence was also the beginning of all things, *ergo*, Intelligence is the beginning and the end, and the circle is complete. This is proved as follows; a circle is traced by ascent and descent: descent is the attribute of the Simple Nature, and ascent the attribute of Compound Bodies; descent resides in Parents, ascent in Offspring; but both the Parents and the Offspring originated with Primal Intelligence, therefore Intelligence is both the beginning and the end, it refers alike to origin and return, to birth and dissolution, it refers to the Night of Power[1], and to the Day of Resurrection. Again, descent, the remoter it is from the origin, the coarser it becomes, and ascent, the remoter it is from the origin, the more refined it becomes; now the Primal Intelligence caused the descent of the lower world, and the ascent of the higher; therefore the former is much coarser than the latter; but they are still one and the same nature. But their nature originated from the Nature of God, therefore the true conclusion is that the Nature of God first was, and first returned, but was still the same Nature of God. "From Him was the origin, and to Him is the return" (cf. Cor. capp. 10, v. 4, &c.).

and the four elements. They are called *'Abá i haftána,* "the sevenfold sires," and *Ummát i Chahárgána,* "the fourfold mothers."

[1] The night on which the command *Kun* went forth, it is equivalent to the Chaos of the Mosaic cosmogony.

Some say that the originator of the Intelligences of the lower world constitutes a tenth world, and call it the Intelligence of the Lunar Sphere, the Active Intelligence, or the Bestower of Form. Most philosophers, however, agree that there are ten Intelligences of the higher world, all active and originators of the Intelligences and souls of the lower world. The difference in the Intelligence of mankind is from this cause; Intelligences and Souls constitute the higher world, and the fixed stars and planets are their administrators in the lower world; through their influence, therefore, the differences observable in mankind are in proportion to the differences existing between the various Souls and Intelligences of the higher world, and the differences existing between the fixed stars and the planets themselves. Now the various qualities of the last are innumerable; astrologers have discovered some of the properties of the seven planets, but no one can give any clue to those of the fixed stars.

Degrees of Intelligences in the higher world

occasion degrees of Intelligence among mankind

Many of the differences of temperament observable among mankind are owing also to the influence of the seasons; accident of birth, health, fortune, longevity and the like again, are all considered as due to the influence of the Higher World; the method and means by which this influence is exerted is too mysterious and incomprehensible to be discussed.

Other Influences.

In chapter 62, v. 7, of the Coran we find the words, "To God belong the treasuries of the Heaven and the Earth;" these are then of two kinds, heavenly

The treasuries of the Universe.

4

and earthly. To the first class belong the heavens
and the stars, every one of which is a treasury; to
the second class of these treasuries belong earth, air,
fire, and water; every plant and every animal, nay,
every embryo, is a treasury in itself. "Verily there
is nothing of which the treasury is not with Us."
(Cor. cap. 15, v. 21). The treasuries of Heaven and
Earth are countless; they may be called the Hosts
of the Lord, as the Coran has it, "Verily to God
belong the Hosts of the Heavens and the Earth."
(Cor. cap. 48, v. 4.)

CHAPTER V.

OF THE FOUR UNIVERSAL SOURCES[1].

Division
of the
Universe
into four
Sources.

THE Sufis and Unitarians divide the Universe into
four Sources, of which the first is the Nature of God;
the second, the Constructive Spirit; and the third
and fourth are the Invisible and Sensible Worlds.
This division is contrary to the doctrines contained
in the Coran and the Traditional Law, although
many even of the strictest Mollahs recognize it.
These last say, however, that the First Source, that is,
God, created the other three out of nothing, and
will, when it pleases Him, reduce them to nothing
again. The Unitarians maintain that it is impossible
for that which is not, to be, and for that which is,
not to be. That which exists, must ever exist, and
that which exists not, can never exist.

[1] The Persians call them ﺩﺭﻳﺎﻫﺎ "seas."

How then, ask the Sufis, was the world made manifest? And the Unitarians reply as follows.

The First Source, which is God, is a hidden trea-sure, and He desired to be known[1]. He therefore appeared, coming from internal to external being; this was the beginning of the Second Source or Constructive Spirit. This again appeared, and the third and fourth Sources were in like manner made manifest; they are the Invisible and Sensible Worlds. The manner in which these came into being, and from them all material objects, has been narrated in a previous chapter. Everything therefore proceeds from the First Source. The Source then which was a hidden treasure was the internal Nature of God, and every existent being a manifestation of His nature; consequently everything which exists is the nature of God, and there neither is nor can be any other existence save His. *Reconciled with the Unitarian account.*

It was to this doctrine that 'Abdallah ibn 'Abbás[2] referred when he said, " I shall be accused of unbelief if I interpret aright the verse, 'It is God who hath created the seven heavens and of the earth like unto them, and His command descendeth between them, that ye may know that He hath power over all things.'" (Cor. cap. 65, v. 12.) *'Abdallah ibn 'Abbás.*

The Unitarians in general say that these four Sources were always exactly as they are now, and have no precedence whatever, the one over the other. *Precedence of the four Sources.*

[1] Cf. the answer to David's enquiry quoted in p. 5.
[2] One of the companions of Mohammed. Cf. *Hajji Khalfa,* Vol. II. p. 333.

For to assert that any one has such precedence, would be to assume that it must either have been imperfect and grown to perfection, or have been originally perfect and subsequently deteriorated; but any notion of deterioration is incompatible with existence, since that must be the existence of God.

The initiated amongst them, however, allow that the First Source has precedence over the Second, and the Second over the third and fourth; but they state that it is a precedence of order and mind, not of place or time; the precedence of the Sun's Orb over its rays, or of cause over effect, each having been manifested by the preceding.

Summary of the Unitarian account.

The Unitarian theory may be summed up thus; God is the First Source, He is the hidden treasure who desires to make Himself known; the others are manifestations of the First, and the more manifestations take place, the more the First becomes known.

Sufiistic account.

The Sufis maintain that these four Sources have a precedence the one over the other, both of time and place; such precedence as Adam has over Mohammed. The origin of the Universe is placed by them in Eternity (*azal*); that of the Constructive Spirit, the Second Source from which it sprung, in Eternity of Eternities (*azal i azál*), whilst the Nature of God, the First Source, is Sempiternal (*lam yazul wa lá yuzál*).

The Traveller then must overcome the restraints of time and place, before his footsteps can border on the threshold of Eternity.

There are other Unitarians, who explain the Four Sources as follows.

The First Source, the Nature of God, they call an Infinite and Illimitable Light, a boundless and fathomless sea. The Second Source, the Constructive Spirit, proceeding from Him, is likewise an Infinite and Illimitable Light and a boundless and fathomless sea; it comprises and comprehends every existent atom, and governs and administers the entire Universe. The remaining two sources are manifestations of this Infinite Light, and the recurring phenomena of nature are but continued manifestations of the same.

Another Unitarian account.

> The varied pictures I have drawn on space,
> Behold what fair and goodly sights they seem!
> One glimpse I gave them of my glorious face,
> And lo! 'tis now the universal theme.

In this the Unitarian account differs little from the Sufiistic; but the former say that the sole object of such manifestation was that God, the hidden treasure, might make Himself known. It is as it were the mirror of God; the mirror in which His majesty and perfection is reflected, the mirror in which He sees Himself.

The Universe the Mirror of God.

> Look not askance, the Holy one will ever be the same,
> The God of all, though oft invoked by many a different name.

The Universe is the mirror of God, and the heart of man is the mirror of the Universe; if the Traveller then would know God, he must look into his own heart; if he would know the light, he must look into his own heart. In short, if he desire to avoid sin and ignorance, and to attain to holiness and wisdom, the guide that shall conduct him on his path is there, " a still small voice," that ever bids him " eschew the evil and choose the good."

All the earth I'd wandered over seeking still the beacon light,
Never tarried in the daytime, never sought repose at night ;
Till I heard a reverend preacher all the mystery declare,
Then I looked within my bosom, and 'twas shining brightly there.

PART III.

CHAPTER I.

THE SAINTLY AND PROPHETIC OFFICES DEFINED.

MOHAMMED said, "The first thing which God created was my soul," and again, "My soul was the Primal Element;" the two therefore are identical.

Duplicate function of the Primal Element.

Now the Primal Element, it has been already stated, has two functions, namely, that of receiving from God, and that of conveying to the world. The first is called the Saintly, the second is called the Prophetic, and is the manifestation of the other. But as it has been shewn that the Primal Element and Mohammed are identical, it follows that these offices are both vested in him. The Sufis, therefore, believe that Mohammed was a prophet before the creation, and that he holds the office still, although he has left the world; and this opinion is in conformity with his own words, "I was a prophet while Adam was yet betwixt Earth and Clay," and again, "There is no prophet after me."

Sheikh Sa'ad uddin Hamawí, who has been before quoted, says that each of the functions of the Primal

In whom vested.

Element requires an exponent. The exponent of the Prophetic function was Mohammed, and he is the Seal of the Prophets. The exponent of the Saintly function is Mehdí, the last of the Imáms[1], who is yet to come. Up to the present time the Prophetic Office has been manifested, and assumed a definite form, and the particulars thereof are known; the particulars of the Saintly Office cannot become known, nor can it assume a definite form till the appearance of Mehdí, who will be the saint (Welí), as Mohammed was the Prophet (Nebí).

Mehdí the last of the Imáms.

Hitherto the discussions in the schools have been concerning the duties imposed by prophecy, and the particulars of the revelation introduced by it; on the appearance of Mehdí Prophecy, will have been completed, and the era of Saintship commenced. When the duties and particulars of this are known, they will form the subject of discussion until this era also shall have been completed by the appearance of the Day of Resurrection. Then shall the faithful behold the Lord face to face, according to the promise, "Verily, ye shall behold your Lord on the Day of Resurrection, even as ye behold the Sun and the Moon."

[1] Also called *Sahibu'zzemán*, "The Lord of Time." He is to be the sovereign of the world, to bear the name of Mohammed, and introduce the Millennium. Many religious enthusiasts of the Muslems have claimed to be the Sahibu'zzemán, amongst them Ali Mohammed, alias Báb el Islám (the door of Islamism), who founded the sect of the Babis in Persia during the present century. A history of the movement is given by Mirza Kazem-Beg in the *Journal Asiatique*, No. 26. Paris, 1866.

PART IV.

CHAPTER I.

ON THE INFLUENCE OF EARLY PREJUDICE UPON BELIEF.

THE influence and example of parents and teachers are paramount in the formation of the character, and in nothing is this more conspicuous than in the matter of religious belief. Doctrines mistily blended with the earliest recollections of life, daily inculcated as truths by those on whose wisdom and affection the child instinctively and implicitly relies, surrounded by a halo of sanctity that he has been ever taught to regard with awe and veneration, to sully which by the slightest breath of doubt he has been led to believe the deadliest of sins, doctrines such as these become in after years part and parcel of the nature of the man, and are not to be lightly cast aside for systems more attractive to the reason or the sense.

Influence of Parents and Teachers.

The Traveller who has been so trained will confess, and unreservedly believe, the principles of

Its practical effects.

his religion, and will act up to the practice of it, with more conscientious earnestness than he who at the outset of his journey constructs a scheme for himself upon the basis of his elders' counsel, or the conclusions of his own unaided reasoning powers.

Its insufficiency without evidence and Grace. Early prejudice is an external influence, and that which is external is far more practical and active than that which is internal. For which cause much earnestness and devotion and faith in the outward attributes of God is found amongst Travellers of this class, but the light of evidence and Divine Grace is still wanting to make them fully understand that His Knowledge, Will and Power comprehend and pervade the whole range of natural causes and effects.

God as the Causer of Causes. They fail to observe that causes as well as effects yield and are subservient to His will, and attribute every event to the action of some natural law. This class of Travellers will lay great stress upon the efficacy of energy and exertion, and care little for submission and resignation; thus their aspirations are checked by worldly thoughts and desires, and relying upon themselves rather than upon God, they can never hope to attain to a true and full knowledge of Him.

The next class, however, whose early faith has been ripened into conviction by the rays of evidence and proof, recognize God as the Causer of Causes, and relying fully upon Him, rather than upon their own energy and efforts, or upon the things of this world, pass their lives in submission and resignation to His Will. He is their only hope and stay, and the only object of their affections and desires, nor are they ever distracted by the whisperings of doubt or shaken by superstitious fears. If beneath the weight of overpowering misery, or in the intoxication of unwonted prosperity, they should waver for a moment in their belief, they atone for their error by a long and earnest course of penitence and prayer. But when the Traveller has reached that higher Stage where he is illumined by the Divine Grace, then the day of resurrection dawns for him, the earthly clouds roll away, the Heavens are opened, and God in all His glory bursts upon his dazzled view.

Like those of the former class, he confesses with his tongue and believes in his heart, but his faith proceeds not from the precepts of others, or the convictions of his own reason; it flows from a higher source, the fountain-head of grace itself. These are the true Unitarians, for they know and see the Unity of God with a clear and certain eye. They are superior to every consideration, to energy and exertion, to resignation and submission alike, for with them God is all in all. *Faith a Divine gift.*

As a specimen of the arguments by which faith is to be strengthened into conviction, I may instance those of the Unitarians. They maintain that there neither is nor can be any other existence save that of God, and explain this position by a simile thus: Had there never been night, and had men dwelt always in continual day, they would never have known what day really was, but from the constantly recurring contrast of night they can form a *Evidence from analogy.*

clear conception of day; so had there been other
than God, God would have been known, and man
could have formed a clear conception of Him ; but as
he cannot do this, it follows that there is no other
than God. Firdausi, the celebrated author of the
Sháh-náma, says:

> The height and depth of all the world is centered, Lord, in Thee:
> I know not what Thou art, Thou art what Thou alone canst be[1].

The following little parable is also a common-place
with them, and points to the same idea.

THE PARABLE OF THE FISHES.

A parable.   Once upon a time the fishes of a certain river took
counsel together, and said, "They tell us that our
life and being is from the water, but we have never
seen water, and know not what it is." Then some
among them wiser than the rest said : "We have

---

[1] It was this couplet which his enemies made use of when
accusing the poet before Sháh Mahmúd of heresy and Sufiism.
The Sultan in consequence refused Firdausi the full reward which
he had promised him for the composition of his Sháh-náma, and
compelled him to seek safety in flight from Ghazní. This conduct
called forth from Firdausi the spirited satire which is so much ad-
mired in the East, and in which he defends himself as follows :—

> "Men fain would call me infidel or worse,
>   And say that heresy defiles my verse ;
>   And sure no viler caitiff ere was born
>   Than he whose soul religious truths would scorn.
>   They lie! I serve my God and Prophet still;
>   Aye! though a tyrant would my life-blood spill !
>   Ne'er shall my soul from duty's path be led,
>   Not were thy sword uplifted o'er my head."

heard that there dwelleth in the sea a very wise and learned fish who knoweth all things; let us journey to him, and ask him to shew us water, or explain unto us what it is." So several of their number set out upon their travels, and at last came to the sea wherein this sage fish resided. On hearing their request he answered them thus :

> Oh ye who seek to solve the knot!
> Ye live in God, yet know him not.
> Ye sit upon the river's brink,
> Yet crave in vain a drop to drink.
> Ye dwell beside a countless store,
> Yet perish hungry at the door.

Then they thanked him, and said, "Forasmuch as thou hast shown us what water is not, we now know perfectly what it is." And they departed to their own homes satisfied.

Another class of Unitarians maintain that there Life a dream. are, it is true, two existences, but one is real, which is of God, and the other imaginative, which is but a mirage, and a reflection of the real. Thus neither the world nor the vicissitudes of human life have any real existence; they are mere reflections of the existence of God, beheld as it were in the changing diorama of a fleeting dream.

PART V.

THE STUDY OF MAN.

CHAPTER I.

GROUNDS FOR THE DISCUSSION.

"Know thyself." LIKE the ancient sages the Oriental Philosophers hold the maxim "Know thyself," to be one of vital importance to the Traveller on the Road of Life. A considerable portion therefore of their speculative treatises is invariably devoted to the study of mankind.

Religious Much difference of opinion exists as to the point of view from which man is to be discussed; the religious teachers asserting that since God created him from nothing he may be considered as an actual being whose characteristics are capable of diagnosis and definition.

and Metaphysical view of the question. The metaphysicians, on the other hand, say that it is impossible for that which is not, to be, or for that which is, not to be; they allow, however, that that which is may assume various forms and manifest itself in different ways, and prefer considering man as a particular manifestation of the one Uni-

versal existence of God. Both however agree in the
propriety of the discussion, though upon different
grounds.

Man constitutes the Lesser World, and everything Man, a
that is not man is included in the Greater World; world in
himself.
and since every thing in the Greater World has its
counterpart in the Lesser, the study of this is a
duty incumbent upon all who aspire to spiritual
knowledge.   To know oneself is the "right way"
(صراط المستقيم), for guidance in which Mohammed
besought God in his prayer, "Guide us into the right
way[1]."   Self-knowledge is the shortest road to the
knowledge of God.   When Ali asked Mohammed
"What am I to do that I may not waste my time?"
the Prophet answered, "Learn to know thyself."

CHAPTER II.

OF THE ORIGIN AND ANIMAL DEVELOPMENT
OF MAN.

THE Lesser World is the counterpart of the Greater. The
In the Greater World there are four Sources, Sources of
his being.
namely, the nature of God, the Constructive Spirit
(or Primal Element), the Invisible and the Sensible
World.

The nature of God begets, the Constructive Spirit
conceives, and the offspring is the tracts of heaven
and the elements.   The tracts of heaven again beget,
and the elements conceive, and their offspring is the
triple kingdom, Animal, Vegetable, and Mineral.

[1] Coran, opening chapter, v. 5.

In like manner there are four Sources in the Lesser World, namely, male and female generation, and the body and soul of man.

Intelligence his starting point and final aim.

But the Constructive Spirit is identical with Primal Intelligence, therefore when man has attained to intelligence he has completed his upward progress (عرج), and reached the point from which he started; the circle is thus complete. But Intelligence is in direct communication with God; therefore when man has attained to this point he has also attained to God. "From Him is the beginning, and unto Him is the return." The saying of Mohammed, "He who has seen me has seen God," refers to this, and not to any blasphemous assumption of divinity; for we must bear in mind that he is identified by his followers with Primal Intelligence.

Conception.

It is unnecessary here to describe the first germination of the embryo; the curious will find a particular account of it, according to the Mohammedan theory, in Sale's Translation of the Coran, cap. 22, v. 5, and in the Arab commentators upon cap. 96.

Suffice it to say that according to them the cartilages, arteries, and nerves are formed during the first three months after conception; in the fourth month, whilst the sun is in the ascendant, the first germ of life appears; the limbs and members are next formed and nourished by blood, introduced through the placenta, by means of the umbilical cord; these are followed by the successive developments of the body and the soul, which arrive at

Birth.

perfection in the eighth month; in the ninth, when

Jupiter is in the ascendant, the child is born into the world.

The embryo partakes of all four elements, earth, water, air and fire; now these in the Greater World produce a triple offspring, mineral, vegetable and animal. A similar division is therefore made in the human body. The members and limbs which are first formed partake of the four elements in different proportions, and the combined result corresponds to the mineral kingdom. The powers of attraction, contraction, absorption, digestion, rejection, growth and formation, are next developed in the members and limbs, which then require nourishment. This they receive in the shape of blood, introduced through the placenta; the chyme contained in this becoming matured is developed into the vegetative spirit, corresponding to the second division of the three kingdoms. When the digestive and other internal organs have become fully developed, the heart attracts to itself the essence of this vegetative spirit, and having further matured it, forms the life; the essence of this again is attracted to the brain, where, after being matured, it is developed into the soul, and the remainder dispersed through the nerves into the limbs, where it becomes the source of sense and motion. This corresponds to the animal kingdom of the Greater World.

Successive develop-ments.

Each of these developments occupies one month, embryo, mineral, vegetative and animal.

The senses are ten in number, five external and *The senses.*

five internal. The external senses are Sight, Hearing, Taste, Smelling, and Feeling.

The internal senses are the Common Sense (حس مشترك), Imagination (خيال), Apprehension (وهم), Memory (حافظه), and Reflection (متصرفه). The Common Sense is involved in the Imagination, and the Apprehension in the Memory; the two former are situate in the fore-part of the brain, the two latter in the after-part, and the Reflection occupies the middle. The Common Sense is so called from comprising every thing that perceives the outward senses. It comprehends visible objects, while the Apprehension apprehends invisible subjects.

It is the Common Sense which appreciates the real nature of all that the external senses perceive, as for instance, distinguishing a friend from an enemy by the marks of which the external senses take cognizance. The Reflection is that which similarly appreciates the conceptions of the Imagination.

The faculties.

The motive powers are also of two kinds, causative and active. The active powers are subservient to and obey the causative, producing motion and the like at their instigation. The causative powers exercise two distinct functions, namely attraction for the acquirement of pleasure or usefulness, and repulsion for the avoidance of annoyance or harm. The former is called Lust, the latter Indignation.

Hitherto only those qualities of man have been

treated of which he shares in common with the
other animals; his spiritual and intellectual developments require another chapter.

CHAPTER III.

OF THE INTELLECTUAL AND SPIRITUAL DEVELOP-
MENT OF MAN.

EVERY animal possesses a vegetative spirit, a living The Spirit
spirit, and an instinctive spirit; but man has an ad- of Humanity,
ditional inheritance, namely the Spirit of Humanity.
Now this was breathed by God into man directly
from Himself, and is therefore of the same character as the Primal Element : "And when I have
fashioned him and breathed My spirit into him."
(Cor. cap. 15, v. 29). The Sufis do not interpret this
of the Life, but of the Spirit of Humanity, and say
that it is frequently not attained until a late period
of life, thirty or even eighty years. Before man can how ac-
receive this Spirit of Humanity he must be fur- quired;
nished with capacity, which is only to be acquired
by purifying oneself from all evil and immoral qualities and dispositions, and adorning oneself with the
opposite ones. Sheikh Muhíy-uddín ibn ul 'Arabí[1],
in his "Investigations" (فصوص), says that the words
"and when I have fashioned him," refer to this
preparation, and the rest of the sentence, "and
breathed My spirit into him," refers to the accession
of the Spirit of Humanity.

[1] *Fusús el Hikam*, Metaphysical Investigations by Muhíy-uddín
Mohammed ben 'Alí el Hátimí el Táyí ibn el Arabí.

Two conditions are therefore imposed upon the Traveller, first, to attain Humanity, second, to acquire capacity.

There are three developments ·of character that must be suppressed before man can attain to Humanity; the animal, the brutal, and the fiendish. He who only eats and sleeps, and gives way to lust, is mere animal; if besides these he gives way to anger and cruelty, he is brutal; and if in addition to ·all these he is crafty, lying, and deceitful, he is fiendish.

If the Traveller is moderate in his food, rest, and desires, and strives to attain a knowledge of himself and of God, then is the time for acquiring capacity by freeing himself from all that is evil and base, and adorning himself with the opposite qualities; after that by prayer he may obtain the Spirit of Huma- constitutes nity. Some one has truly said that there is none of real im- the perfection, essence, or immortality of man, save mortality. only among such as are "created with a godly dispo- sition." When the Traveller has once been revivi- fied by the Spirit of Humanity he becomes immortal, and inherits everlasting life. This is why it has been said that "man has a beginning but no end."

The Divine   If when he has attained this Spirit of Humanity, Light.   he is earnest, and does not waste his life in trifling, he soon arrives at the Divine Light itself. For "God guideth whom He pleaseth unto His Light." The attainment of this light is the completion of Man's upward progress, but no one can attain to it but those who are pure in spirit and in their lives.

Mohammed asserted that he himself had attained it, "To the light have I reached, and in the light I live;" now this light is the Nature of God; wherefore he said "who seeth me seeth God."

The germ that contains the Primal Element of Man is the lowest of the low, and the Divine Light is the highest of the high; it is between these extremes that the stages of man's upward or downward progress lie. "We have created man in the fairest of proportions, and then have thrown him back to be the lowest of the low, save only such as believe and act with righteousness; and verily these shall have their reward." (Cor. cap. 95, v. 4). This reward is said by the Sufis to be defined by the word *ajrat*, "reward," itself. This word contains three radical letters ا ج and ر; ا stands for اعادة "return," ج for جنّة "paradise" and ر for روية, that is "those who have handed down the faith." Their acting righteously is their return to the Nature of God, for when they have finished their upward progress, and reached this they are in Paradise, and in the presence of their God. He therefore is a man, in the true sense of the word, who being sent down upon earth strives upward towards Heaven. These aspirations are indispensable to man; he might by the Almighty Power of God exist without all beside, even had the Heavens and the elements themselves never been; but these things are the aim and want of all.

It has been said that the Primal Element or constructive spirit as well as the Spirit of Humanity

ity identi-
cal with
the Primal
Element.
proceed direct from God. They are therefore identical, and are both included by the Sufis in the one
term Concomitant Spirit. Now this Spirit, although
distinct and individual, comprehends and governs
the entire Universe. The Simple Natures are its
administrators and exponents ; of these the Seven
Sires beget, and the Four Mothers conceive from the
incarnation of this spirit in them, and their offspring
is the triple kingdom, Mineral, Vegetable, and Animal. And so it is with the Lesser World of Man.

Now this Spirit hath two functions, external and
internal ; the external is revealed in the material
generation just alluded to, the internal abides in the
heart of man. Whosoever purifies his heart from
worldly impressions and desires reveals this internal
function of the Spirit within him, and illumines and
revivifies his soul.

Thus the Spirit at once comprehends the Universe and dwells in the heart of man.

CHAPTER IV.

OF THE UPWARD PROGRESS OR ASCENT OF MAN.

Man's up-
ward Pro-
gress.
WHEN Man has become assured of the truth of
Revelation he has reached the stage of Belief, and
has the name of *Múmin*, "Believer." When he further acts in obedience to the will of God, and appor-
tions the night and day for earnest prayer, he has
reached the stage of worship, and is called an *'Abid*,
or "Worshipper." When he has expelled the love
of this world from his heart, and occupies himself

with a contemplation of the mighty Whole, he reaches
the next stage, and becomes a *Záhid*, or "Recluse."
When in addition to all this he knows God, and subsequently learns the mysteries of nature, he reaches
the stage of Acquaintance, and is called *'Arif*, "One
who knows." The next stage is that in which he
attains to the love of God, and is called a *Welí* or
"Saint." When he is moreover gifted with inspiration and the power of working miracles, he becomes
a *Nebí*, "Prophet;" and when entrusted next with
the delivery of God's own message, he is called an
"Apostle," *Rusúl*. When he is appointed to abrogate
a previous dispensation and preach a new one, he
is called *Ulu 'l 'Azm*, "One who has a mission."
When this mission is final he has arrived at the stage
called *Khatm*, or "the Seal." This is the Upward
Progress of Man. The first stage is the "Believer,"
the last the "Seal."

After separation from the body, the soul of
Man returns to that Heaven which corresponds to
the stage which he has attained; thus the Believer
at last dwells in the first or lowest Heaven, and the
Seal in the Heaven of Heavens; for it will be noticed
that the stages of upward progress correspond to the
number of degrees in the Heavenly Spheres, namely,
seven inferior and two superior. *Destination of the soul,*

The metaphysicians say that these stages and
degrees do not in reality exist, but that the Heavenly Intelligence which corresponds to the degree of
intelligence attained by Man attracts and absorbs
his soul into itself after separation from the body. *metaphysically explained.*

Thus every one who has attained intelligence corresponding to that of the highest sphere, his soul returns thereto ; and he who has attained intelligence corresponding to the lowest sphere, his soul in like manner returns to that ; those who have not attained intelligence corresponding to any of these will be placed in Hell, which is situate below the lowest sphere.

As each of the Heavenly Spheres is furnished with knowledge and purity in proportion to its position, the rank of Man's soul in the future state will, according to this last account, be in proportion to his degree of knowledge and purity of life while upon the earth.

The Upward Progress infinite.

The Unitarians say that man's Upward Progress has no end, for if he strive for a thousand years, each day will teach him something that he knew not before, inasmuch as the knowledge of God has no limit. So Mohammed says, "He who progresses daily is yet of feeble mind."

Simile illustrating the foregoing.

The religious account says that the soul of every man returns to an individual place after separation from the body. This the metaphysicians deny; for how, say they, can the soul of a man return to a certain place when it has not originally come from a certain place? The soul of man is the Primal Spirit, and if a thousand persons live, it is the same spirit that animates them all; and in like manner if a thousand die, the same spirit returns to itself, and is not lessened or diminished. If a myriad persons build houses and make windows therein the same sun illumines them all, and though every one of them should be destroyed, the sun would not be lessened or diminished. The sun is the lord of the sensible world, and the exponent of the attributes of the Primal Spirit. The Primal Spirit is the lord of the invisible world and the exponent of the Nature of God[1].

When the heart of man has been revivified and illumined by the Primal Spirit, he has arrived at Intelligence; for Intelligence is a light in the heart, distinguishing between truth and vanity. Until he has been so revivified and illumined, it is impossible for him to attain to intelligence at all. But having attained to intelligence, then, and not till then, is the time for the attainment of knowledge, for becoming Wise. Intelligence is a Primal Element, and knowledge the attribute thereof. When from knowledge he has successively proceeded to the attainment of the Divine Light, and acquaintance with the mysteries of nature, his last step will be Perfection, with which his Upward Progress concludes.

Intelligence the aim of the Upward Progress.

But dive he ever so deeply into the treasury of

Retrogression how avoided.

[1] The following from Tennyson's *In Memoriam* forms a beautiful protest against the ideas here set forth:

> That each who seems a separate whole
>   Should move his rounds, and fusing all
>   The skirts of self again, should fall
> Remerging in the general soul,
>
> Is faith as vague as all unsweet:
>   Eternal form shall still divide
>   The eternal soul from all beside;
> And I shall know him when we meet.

mysteries and knowledge, unless he examine himself
and confess that after all he knows naught, all that
he has acquired will slip through his hands, and leave
him far poorer than before.   His treasure of to-day
should as much exceed the treasure of yesterday as
an ocean exceeds a drop ; but this can never be, unless he, leaving all else for contemplation and self-
examination, have freedom and leisure to learn how
poor he really is, and how much he needs the saving
help of God.

Unitarian account.   One class of Unitarians explain the Upward Progress of Man thus.   They say that every atom of existent beings is filled with light ;

> Arise and look around, for every atom that has birth
> Shines forth a lustrous beacon to illumine all the earth:

but that man walks abroad in darkness, blinded by
the lusts of life, and laments the want of light that
would, were he but aware of it, involve him in the
glorious sheen of brightest day :

> 'Twere well to catch the odours that about our senses play,
> For all the world is full of blasts to bear the sweets away.

Upward Progress   What they mean is this, that all existent beings are
compounded of two things, darkness and light, which
are indistinguishably blended together.   The light
belongs to the Invisible, and the darkness to the Sensible world ; but the two are intimately connected, and
the former exercises a paramount influence upon the
latter.   The object of man, according to them, is to
separate the light from the darkness, that its nature
and attributes may be understood, and in this consists
his **Upward Progress.**

Although the light and the darkness can never be entirely separated, for the one is as it were the veil of the other, the light can be made to prevail, so that its attributes may become manifest.

Now it is possible to separate thus far the light from the darkness in certain cases; in the bodies of men and animals, for instance, there are certain organs always at work, whose sole object is this separation. Thus, when food is introduced into the stomach, the liver receives the cream and essence of it and transmits it to the heart; the heart, in like manner, extracts the essence of this, which is the life, and transmits it to the brain; lastly, the brain extracts the essence of this, and transforms it into the elixir of life, the real light of all. *consists in the separation of Light and Darkness.*

The elixir evolved by the brain is the instinctive spirit, and is as it were a lamp in a lantern; but it gives forth after all but a flickering and cloudy light, and man's object should therefore be to strengthen and purify it by Renunciation and Contemplation, until it give forth the true light which is the Spirit of Humanity. When man has attained to this he necessarily becomes free from all that is evil, and is adorned instead with every good and noble quality.

The body of man is like a lantern, the Vegetative Spirit is the lamp, the Animal Spirit is the wick, the Instinctive Spirit the oil, and the Spirit of Humanity the fire that kindles all. "Verily its oil would almost shine even though no fire kindled it." (Cor. cap. 24, v. 35). In other words, the Instinctive *Man likened to a lamp.*

Spirit should feed and supply the Spirit of Humanity, as the oil feeds and supplies the flame in a lamp. The Traveller must aim at completing this lamp, so that his heart may be illumined, and he may see things as they really are. When the Spirit of Humanity a "light upon light" (Cor. cap. 24, v. 35) has thus kindled the Instinctive Spirit, God "guideth whom He pleaseth to His own light" (idem), that is, to the divine light of His own nature, reaching which the Traveller's Upward Progress is complete ; for "from Him they spring, and unto Him return."

CHAPTER V.

CONCLUSION.

Summary. THE words quoted in the first chapter, "I am a hidden treasure, and I would fain be known," form the basis of the whole system of Sufiistic speculation. Considering the entire universe merely as a manifestation of God, produced by the agency of intelligence directly proceeding from Him, they rightly surmise that this intelligence is the only means by which He can be known.

Now man being with them the most perfect entity in the universe, is clearly the instrument by which the object of its creation is to be accomplished ; but this object is that God should be known, and He can only be known through intelligence ; therefore the attainment of.this intelligence is the final aim of man.

But as man sprung from the Intelligence which originated the Universe, and should, as has been just stated, tend to the same, the Sufis proceed to consider his existence as a circle meeting in the Intelligence which reveals the Godhead. This circle they divide into two arcs, the former called Descent (*nuzúl*), includes every stage, from the first scintillation from the original intelligence to the full development of man's reasoning powers; the latter arc, called Ascent (*'urúj*), includes every stage, from his first use of reason for its true purpose to his final reabsorption into the Divine intelligence. This is what is meant when they speak of the Origin and Return of Man. Development of the system.

The Ascent, or upward progress, naturally presents itself to the Sufiistic mind in the form of a journey, and the doctrines which profess to describe it are accordingly called the road (*taríkat*). Idea of the "Journey."

When a man possessing the necessary requirements of fully developed reasoning powers turns to them for a resolution of his doubts and uncertainties concerning the real nature of the Godhead, he is called a *Tálib*, or Searcher after God. The *Tálib*, or Neophyte.

If he manifest a further inclination to prosecute his inquiry according to their system, he is called a *Muríd*, or One who inclines. The *Muríd* or Disciple.

Placing himself then under the spiritual instruction of some eminent leader of the sect, he is fairly started upon his journey, and becomes a *Sálik* or Traveller, whose whole business in after-life is *sulúk*, devotion, (or, as the word signifies, the prosecution The *Sálik*, or Traveller.

of his journey,) to the end that he may ultimately arrive at the knowledge of God.

1st stage, Worship.

Here he is exhorted to serve God as the first step towards a knowledge of Him; this is the first stage of his journey, and is called '*Abúdiyat*, Service or Worship.

2nd stage, Love.

When in answer to his prayers the Divine influence or Attraction has developed his inclination into love of God, he is said to have reached the stage called '*Ishk*, Love.

3rd stage, Seclusion.

This Divine Love expelling all worldly desires from his heart, leads him to the next stage, called *Zuhd*, or Seclusion.

4th stage, Knowledge.

Occupying himself henceforward with contemplations and the investigations of those metaphysical theories concerning the nature, attributes, and works of God, which have been described in the Second Part of this treatise, he reaches his next stage, which is that of *Ma'rifat*, Knowledge.

5th stage, Ecstasy.

Now this assiduous contemplation of startling metaphysical theories is exceedingly attractive to an Oriental mind, and not unfrequently produces a state of mental excitement akin to the phenomena observed during the recent religious revivals. Such ecstatic state is considered a sure prognostication of direct illumination of the heart by God, and constitutes the next stage, *Wejd* or *Hál*, Ecstasy.

6th stage, Truth.

During this stage he is supposed to receive a revelation of the true nature of the Godhead, and to have reached the stage called *Hakíkat*, or The Truth.

He is then said to proceed to the stage of *Jam'* 7th stage, or *Wasl*, direct Union with God. Union.

Further than this he cannot go, but pursues his Last habit of self-denial and contemplation until his death, stage, Extinction. which is, however, merely looked upon as a total reabsorption into the Deity, forming the consummation of his Journey, the last stage designated *Faná*, Extinction.

That stage in which he is said to have attained The Interto the Love of God is the point of view from which pretation of Mystical the Sufiistic poets love to discuss the doctrines of Poems. their sect; with them man is the Lover, God the Beloved One, and the journey above described is referred to allegorically as the distance which separates the lover from the object of his affection. The glossary which I have appended to this work will enable the student of Háfiz and other Sufiistic writers to interpret for himself the Mystical Poems of the East.

Thus far have we followed the Traveller upon his trackless path through every mystery, human and divine. But one thing now remains; if we, like him, aspire to reach the goal we must cast away the pride of intellect and boasted knowledge, and kneeling before the throne of God in humble thankfulness for the light He hath already vouchsafed, ask Him for guidance and protection who alone is "the light and life of men."

APPENDIX.

GLOSSARY

OF TECHNICAL AND ALLEGORICAL EXPRESSIONS
IN USE AMONG THE SÚFÍ POETS.

(A. *Arabic.* P. *Persian.*)

P.   ابرو   *abrú.* The eyebrow. The miracles of Moses.

A.   اجتماع   *ijtimá'.* Collection. Man's sole desire being concentrated in a longing after God.

A.   اسفار   *asfár.* Journeys. There are four journeys undertaken by the Súfí Traveller. 1. The journey to God. See Part I. Chapter I. 2. The journey to God whilst journeying in God. 3. The upward progress and actual meeting with the Deity. 4. The journey to God whilst journeying from God for the recovery of sinners.

A.   اسلام   *islám.* Islamism. Resignation. Submission to the decrees of God.

A.   اُلست   *alast.* "Art thou not?" The words uttered by the voice of God, "Art thou not My creature?" See *nidá.*

A.   انانيت   *anániyat.* Egotism.

6

P.   انگشت   *angusht.* Finger. God's all-compre-
hending power.

A.   ایمان   *imán.* Faith. Finding God.

P.   آینه   *á'ina.* Mirror. The human heart. Mir-
rors in the East were of metal, hence
the frequent occurrence of such expressions as "polish thy mirror,"
meaning "purify thy heart."

P.   باده   *báda.* New wine. Divine love.

P.   بازو   *bázú.* Arm. God's Will.

A.   باطل   *bátil.* False. All that is not God.

P.   بامداد   *bámdád.* Morning. The last stage of
the journey.

P.   بت   *but.* Idol. God as the object of contemplation.

P.   بت‌پرست   *but parast.* Idol-worshipper. A con-
templative devotee.

A.   بیت‌الحرام   *baitu 'l harám.* The Holy of Holies.
In Sufi poetry it represents the Per-
fect Man.

A.   بیت‌المقدس   *baitu 'l mucaddas.* The House of Holiness. Ordinarily used to designate
the Temple at Jerusalem, but in Sufiistic language, a heart unpolluted by
earthly love.

P.   پاکبازي   *pákbází.* Purity. Inclination towards holiness without expecting reward or promotion, but rather seeking after God for His own sake.

P.   پدر   *peder.* Father. God's purpose of revelation.

P.   پیشاني   *peshání.* Forehead. The path of inquiry into the mysteries of a future state. See *hablu 'l matín.*

A.   تجلّي   *tajallí.* Appearance. Every mystery that is revealed to the heart.

P.   ترسا   *tarsá.* Pagan. The revelation of God's majesty. See *jemál.*

P.   ترسانچه   *tarsá-bachcha.* A young Pagan. The Germ of the state called Hál, q. v.

A.   تصوّف   *tasawwuf.* Sufiism. The purification (*tasfíyeh*) of the heart from earthly mists. See *áina.*

A.   تفرقه   *tafrikah.* Distraction. Pondering upon God's general disposition and arrangement in the universe.

A.   توحيد   *tauhíd.* Unity. The Nature of God.

P.   جان   *ján.* Soul. Darling. The manifestations of the Beloved (God).

P.   جانان   *jánán.* Darling of darlings. A constant mistress. God, the concentration of stability.

A.   جاهل   *jáhil.* Ignorant. Worldly.

A.   جذبه   *jazbah.* Attraction. The nearer approach of man to his Maker, through His Grace.

A.   جرع   *jar'.* A draught. The mysteries of the various stages of the journey, or, according to some, everything that is hidden from the disciple's understanding during his prosecution of the journey (سلوك).

A.   جلال   *jalál.* Majesty. That which veils God from human sight.

A.   جمال   *jamál.* Beauty. Manifestation of the Majesty oi the Beloved One (God).

A.   جمع   *jam'.* Collection. The unity of God.

A.   جمع‌الجمع   *jam 'u 'l jam'.* In Arabic grammar the plural of a plural. The high position of the Perfect Man.

P.   چاہ‌زنخ   *cháh i zanakh.* A dimple in the chin. The secret mystery of beholding God.

P.   چشم   *chashm.* The eye. The beauty of Joseph.

A.   حج   *hajj.* Pilgrimage. The prosecution of the journey by devotion alone. See Part I. Chapter IV.

A.   حال   *hál.* State. Ecstasy. The beatific state induced by continued contemplation of God. This is considered to be a divine gift, and a sure prognostication of speedily arriving at The Truth.

A.   حبل المتين   *hablu 'l matín.* The strong rope. Acknowledging the Unity of God.

A.   حسن   *husn.* Beauty. The concentration of perfection in One Nature.

A.   حكمت   *hikmat.* Wisdom. Metaphysics. Comprehension of the mysteries of Nature.

A.   حق   *Hacc.* The Truth. God.

A.   حقيقت   *hakíkat.* Truth. Determination of the Nature of God.

A.   حقيقة الحقايق   *hakíkatu 'l haká-ik.* Truth of Truths. The Nature of God as comprising all truth.

P.   خال سياه   *khál i siyáh.* A black mole (considered a great beauty in the East). The future state.

P.   خرابات   *kharábát.* Tavern. The stage in which the Traveller is immersed in the Divine mysteries.

A.   خرقه   *khirkah.* The patched and ragged garment of a religious recluse. Comeliness and soundness of principle.

A.P. خط سبز *khatt i sabz.* Verdure. Down just appearing upon the cheek. The state of limbo, *barzakh* (cf. Sale's Coran, chap. xxiii. note u).

A. خلایق *khalá-ik.* Tempers. Peoples. God's attribute of Power.

P. خم زلف *kham i zulf.* A twisting curl. Joy of the heart at knowing God[1].

P. خواهر *kh'áhar.* Sister. Revelation.

A. داخل وخارج *dákhil u khárij.* Entrance and exit. Drunkenness and Intoxication, see *masti.*

P. دست *dast.* Hand. God's attribute of Power.

A. دقیقه *dakíkah.* Tittle. Probation.

A. دنیا *dunyá.* The world. Anything that hinders man from seeking after God.

A. دیر *dair.* Monastery. The world of Humanity.

---

[1] Tholuck in his SUFISMUS (Berolini, MDCCCXXI), p. 105, explains this as follows: "*Cincinnorum circuli,* Sic divina dicunt mysteria, nemini præter Deum ipsum nota." This, however, is the interpretation of *zulf* (tresses), not *kham i zulf.* The verse quoted above, in page 41,

"One glimpse I gave them of my glorious face,"

affords a good illustration of this. The words of the original being

سر موی ز زلف خود نمودیم

"I showed them a hair's point of my *tresses* (*zulf*)."

A. دین   *dín.* Religion. Belief arising from the stage called *tafrikah,* q. v.

P. دهان   *dahán.* Mouth. An attribute of God as speaking with man.

P. رخسار   *rukhsár.* The cheek. Cosmos.

P. رندي   *rindí.* Profligacy. Thinking no more of human conventionalities.

P. روزه   *rúza.* Fasting. The stage called *wasl* (q. v.), in which the Traveller abandons the world.

P. روي   *rúy.* Face. The manifestation of the Deity as comprehending all things. Also The Mirror in which the Godhead is reflected. See Part II. Chap. 5.

A. زاهد   *záhid.* A Recluse.

P. زلف   *zulf.* Tresses. The mystery of the Godhead.

A. زنار   *zunnár.* The sacred Cord worn by the Magi. The Brahminical Thread. A mistress' ringlet; hence allegorically by the Sufis, the yearning after the appearance of the Beloved One (God).

P. زنخ   *zanakh.* The chin. The point at which one beholds God.

A. زهد   *zuhd.* Abstinence. Forsaking the outer world and giving oneself up entirely to contemplation.

A.   ساعد   *sá 'id.* Arm. God's attribute of Might.

A.   ساقي   *sákí.* Cupbearer. The appearance of Divine Love which calls for thankfulness.

P.   سخن   *sukhan.* Speech. The warnings of God.

A.   سفر   *safr.* A journey. Turning the attention towards God.

A. سوادالوجةفي الدارين   *sawád u'l wajhi fi 'd dárain.* Blackening the face (i.e. disgrace) in both worlds. Complete self-denial implying the state of him who performs the last of the "four journeys" described under *asfar.*

P.   شاهد   *sháhid.* Mistress. The appearance of The Truth (God).

P.   شبانگاه   *shabángáh.* A Night lodging. The last stage on the Journey.

A.   شراب   *sharáb.* Drink, Wine. The domination of Divine Love over the heart.

A. P. شرابخانه   *sharáb khána.* Wine shop. The invisible world.

A.   شمع   *sham'.* Candle. The Divine Light kindling the torch of the Traveller. See *candíl.*

P.   شور   *shor.* Disturbance. Noise. Intercourse between God and man.

A.   شهود   *shuhúd.* Gaze. The unobstructed vision of the Godhead.

A.   صبا   *sabá.* The Zephyr. The breathings of the Spirit.

A.   طاعت   *tá'at.* Obedience. Righteousness. The Knowledge of God.

A.   عارف   *'árif.* Knowing. One gifted by God with a thorough knowledge of His Nature, Works and Attributes.

A.   عاشق   *'áshik.* Lover. Man.

A.   عالم‌جبروت   *á'lam i jubrút.* The World of Powers. The names and attributes of God. The visible, invisible and future worlds.

A.   عشرت   *'ishrat.* Pleasure. Joy in the Lord.

A.   غار   *ghár.* A hollow. Jealousy. Turning the heart towards God.

A.   غمّاز   *ghammáz.* One who throws side glances. The turning of the heart towards God.

A.   فراغت   *firághat.* Rest. Devotion to things of this world.

A.   فراق   *firák.* Separation. Not recognizing the unity of God.

A.   فنا   *faná.* Vanishing. The total annihilation of self in the contemplation of God.

A.   فناي‌تمام   *faná e tamám.* Complete disappearance. Total annihilation and absorption of self in the contemplation of God. Death.

A.   قاتل   *cátil.* Slayer. The first manifestation of desire on the part of man and of attraction on the part of God.

A.   قتیل   *catíl.* Slain (as by the arrows of a mistress' glance). Acceptable to God.

A.   قدح   *cadh.* Goblet. Time.

A.   قلب   *calb.* Heart. The intermediate state between the illumination of the reason and the soul by the Divine Light.

A.   قندیل   *candil.* Torch or Candle. The heart of the Traveller kindled by Divine Love.

A.   کافر   *káfir.* Unbeliever. One who has reached the stage called *tafrikah,* q.v.

A.   کبر   *kibr.* Haughtiness. The grandeur of God.

A.   کتاب مبین   *kitáb i mubín.* The perspicuous book. In the Coran it signifies the contents of the eternal tablet on which that revelation was inscribed and which is also called لوح. With the Sufis it stands for the heart of the Perfect Man.

A.   کعبه   *ka'ba.* The Temple at Mecca, to which the Mohammedans turn their faces in prayer. The state called *wasl,* q.v.

A.   کفر   *kufr.* Unbelief. The darkness of the stations on the road.

P.   کنار   *kinár.* Embrace. Discovery of the mysteries of the Godhead.

P. گوش   *gúsh.* Ear. Capacity for receiving the words of God by pursuing knowledge. Sometimes it means knowledge itself, exoteric and esoteric.

P. گیسو   *gísú.* Ringlet. Details of the mysteries of divinity.

A. لاهوت   *láhút.* Divinity. Life permeating all things.

A. لبّ   *lubb.* Pith. Intelligence sanctified and purified from doubts and suspicions.

P. لب لب   *lab lab.* Brimful. Drinking in the Light of God and having the gaze riveted upon Him.

P. A. لب لعل   *lab i lá'l.* A ruby lip. The unheard but understood words of God[1]. Conscience.

A. مادر   *mádar.* Mother. The tablets on which the Coran is said to have been inscribed from all eternity; called by the Arabs امّ الكتاب *ummu 'l Kitáb,* "The Mother of The Book."

A. مثال   *misál.* Fiction. The stage in which the Traveller arrives at a Comprehension of the unity of God.

A. مخموري   *makhmúrí.* Drunkenness. Returning from the stage called *wusúl* (see *wasl*), by way of cessation.

---

[1] Cf. the answer of the Delphic oracle to Crœsus, Herod. I. 47. 4:
καὶ κωφοῦ συνίημι, καὶ οὐ φωνεῦντος ἀκούω.

A.   مراقبه   *murákibeh.* Observation. Rejecting conventionalities, and penetrating deeply into the truths of Religion.

P.   مرگ   *marg.* Death. Eternal life. "*Mors janua vitae.*"

A.   مزيد   *mazíd.* Increase. The state of man.

A.   مستي   *mastí.* Intoxication. Escaping from the domination of Love.

A.   مطرب   *mutrib.* Musician. The *pir* or elder who expounds the laws of God to his disciples.

A.   معشوق   *ma'shúk.* The beloved one. God.

P.   مغان   *Mughán.* Magians. Christian monks, confounded with fire-worshippers by the Mohammedans. See *tarsá.*

P.   مغ بچه   *mugh-bachcha.* Young Magian. See *tarsá bachcha.*

A.   مغني   *mughní.* Independent. Confessing the unity of God.

A.   ملحد   *mulhid.* Heretic. Pedant. Being learned in Theology.

A.   موافق   *muwáfik.* Complaisant. See *mulhid.*

P.   ميان   *miyán.* Middle. Waist. The state of the Traveller when nothing remains to veil from him the Glories of God.

P.   ميخانه   *mai khána.* Tavern. The dominion of Divine Love.

P.   میکده   *maikedeh.* Wine-house. That stage of the journey in which inclination is developed into love by the effect of prayer (see Part I. Chap. v.).

A.   ناهوت   *náhút.* The channel through which *láhút* flows, q. v.

A.   نبوت   *nabúwat.* Prophecy. Knowing and proclaiming the truths of Godhead.

A.   ندا   *nidá.* Voice. The voice of God calling in the heart and constituting Attraction. See *jazba.*

A.   وجد   *wajd.* Ecstasy. See *hál.*

A.   وصل   *wasl.* Meeting. The unity of God; also the mean between the external and the internal. Seeing God face to face.

A.   وقت   *wakt.* Time. Fixing the thoughts upon mortality.

A.   ولایت   *wiláyat.* Saintship. Perseverance in the contemplation of God. See *faná;* see also Part III. Chapter I.

A.   ولی   *welí.* Saint. One who has given himself up entirely to contemplation. See *faná.*

A.   هوا   *hawá.* Desire. A yearning after the future life kindled by God in the heart man.

(Greek).   هیولا   *hayúla.* Ἡ ὕλη. Materials. First principles.

INDEX.